Preface

The "Oracle Certified Master Java Enterprise Architect (OCMJEA) (Paper Code - 1Z0-807)" certification represents the highest level of achievement for professionals in Java enterprise architecture. It validates not only technical expertise but also strategic thinking, leadership, and the ability to design scalable, secure, and high-performance enterprise applications. This book serves as a comprehensive guide for OCMJEA aspirants, offering deep insights into architectural patterns, enterprise integration, security, scalability, and performance optimization. Through a blend of theoretical concepts, real-world case studies, and industry best practices, it equips candidates with the knowledge and skills required to architect complex enterprise solutions that align with modern business needs.

Beyond exam preparation, this book fosters a mindset of innovation and adaptability, emphasizing the critical interplay between technology, business requirements, and architectural principles. By instilling a holistic approach to enterprise architecture, it empowers readers to anticipate industry challenges, embrace emerging technologies, and drive digital transformation within organizations. Our hope is that this guide not only helps you achieve OCMJEA certification but also inspires you to become a visionary leader in enterprise architecture, shaping the future of Java-based solutions with confidence and expertise.

Table of Contents

OCMJEA Practice Questions

1. Your company requires all its developers to use a well-specified set of exception classes to model several common error conditions, many of the which are specific to its business. These exception classes are centrally maintained and come packaged in a library (a JAR file). The application you are developing needs to report a number of error conditions covered by this library to remote clients. Which paring of component type and remote access technology enables client applications to use the predefined exceptions as part of their natural programming model?

A. Servlet accessed using HTTP

B. Entity bean accessed using web services

C. Stateless session bean accessed using Remote Method Invocation (RMI)

D. Message-driven bean accessed using Java Message Service (JMS) queue

Answer: C

2. An investment company has purchased a number of small online business referral systems that appeal to various niche demographics. The company wants to bring these networks together in hopes of finding a broad, single theme and brand image for these groups before they can do that, they need to get the users communicating with outside their current networks. Which Web Services pattern would you recommend they consider in building a scheme to accommodate this communication?

A. Asynchronous Interactions

B. PAOS Interactions

C. Web Services Broker

D. JMS Bridge

Answer: A

3. A successful web application is used by over two hundred thousand users. Due to this substantial load, the database is over bridged and fails frequently. Al data, included critical user records and temporary session data, is stored in the database. Because of resource constraints, a new database system cannot be installed. Which change will reduce the load on the database?

A. Creating more entity beans to optimize interaction wild the database

B. Refactoring the web application to use DAOs to communicate with the database

C. Refactoring the web application to store temporary session data on the web servers

D. Adding more web servers to the web tier to distribute the load and reduce the number of transactions on the database.

Answer: C

4. MedLabML is a startup firm that moves patient data between different care providers to provide a "single patient view". They use a B2B system to exchange electronic business document with their key suppliers. They are seeking your advice about standards to review for improving their message-level security. Which standard or API would you recommend they read?

A. SAML 1.1

B. Web Service Interoperability Technology

C. XML Signature

D. SSL

Answer: B

5. A Hot Potato anti pattern can arise from misuse of which technology combination?

A. Bean Validation with JSF Managed Beans

B. Messaging in the Business Tier

C. JNDI Lookups with Global Java Naming

D. JPA with the Web Tier

Answer: C

6. You have been tasked with improving the availability of an existing three tier application. What is your first stop in evaluating what changes should be made to the architecture to achieve the goal?

A. Monitor network traffic between tiers.

B. Separate presentation from business logic.

C. Identify and document all single points of failure.

D. Cluster the presentation tier without session replication.

Answer: C

7. While analyzing an existing web application, you observe the following issues in the source code: Duplicate control code is scattered throughout various view. Business and presentation logic are mixed within this view. The next phase of the project involves refactoring the existing code to address these two issues. Which design pattern, if employed in the refactoring exercise, would most directly address the two issues?

A. Service to Worker

B. Dispatcher view

C. DAO

D. Composite View

Answer: A

8. You are using an open source integration framework in your project. However, key interfaces do not explicitly define several strange conditions you have repeatedly seen while testing. Which option is the name given to the anti-pattern described above?

A. Composite View

B. Leaky Abstraction

C. Asynchronous Interaction

D. Golden Hammer

Answer: C

9. Your development team wants to use Google Guice. A previous architect assigned this request a low priority, citing the complexity of integration and no compel ing benefits statements from the requesting team. The team claims that their colleagues have achieved the integration using a pattern. This pattern reduced the level of difficulty and risk and did not require vendor support. Which pattern fits this description?

A. Context Holder

B. Service Starter

C. Dependency Injection Extender

D. Bean Locator

Answer: C

10. Which statements are true about Java integration technologies?

A. Remote Method Invocation (RMI) helps to connect subsystems in a loosely coupled manner.

B. Java Message Service (JMS) helps in synchronous messaging between Java and non-Java systems.

C. JMS helps to broadcast messages to multiple Java-based receivers.

D. Java Connector Architecture (JCA) helps to integrate with heterogeneous legacy enterprise information systems.

Answer: C

11. Which two statements are true about security strategies at the message level?

A. Messages are secured during transport and after arrival at their destination

B. Each portion of a compound message is secured.

C. SSL is required to ensure authenticity, integrity, and confidentiality.

D. Message attachments are secured without the need for a dedicated API.

E. Security is dependent on the application environment or the transport protocol.

Answer: C, E

12. Which two features are supported by the Java Authentication and Authorization Service (JAAS) API?

A. single sign on

B. secure network connections

C. configurable access control policies

D. web services security

E. message encryption and key generation

Answer: A, C

13. A company manufactures widgets for sale to distribution. Distributors call this company when they want to order more widgets. The company wants the distributors to send orders using XML documents over the Internet to reduce the number of data entry personnel needed. It has no control

over the distributor's technologies. The company does not want the Orders to impact the performance of other users. You have been assigned the task of designing a new API. Which method do you use?

A. Design the API as a Java Message Service (JMS) queue.

B. Design the API as a Remote Method Invocation (RMI) interface.

C. Design the API as a synchronous web service.

D. Design the API as an asynchronous web service.

Answer: D

14. You are the architect of an existing project. Making changes to one component frequently requires making changes to many other components. Which action would reduce future maintenance costs?

A. Redesign the configuration and deployment.

B. Add an abstraction layer between the servlets and the EJB components.

C. Convert all stateful EJB components to stateless EJB components.

D. Expose the existing EJB components as web services.

Answer: B

15. A company has been soiling a desktop based billing application that has Character User Interface (CUI) application developed by using Java. The company would like to release the next version of this application with the following features: a GUI with a pluggable look- and-feel capability and the flexibility to support multiple database vendors. Which two technologies would you use in the new version?

A. Swing

B. JDBC

C. JPA

D. CMP

E. AWT

Answer: A, B

16. An online library wants to introduce a feature where an email notification is generated whenever a book becomes available for circulation. This notification must be sent to only those members who have expressed interest in that book. Which design pattern would you use to implement this requirement?

A. Observer

B. Payload Extractor

C. Asynchronous Resource Integrator

D. Web Service Broker

E. Service Starter

Answer: A

17. Your consulting company has been asked to enhance an existing application. The current application is a two-tier system in which all the business logic is located in thick clients. You are considering a solution that would involve moving the business logic into the server's database. In the form of stored procedures. Which statement is an expected outcome of your proposed solution?

A. It will improve the scalability of the system.

B. It will improve the manageability of the system.

C. It will recline the amount of traffic on the network.

D. It will in effect, turn the application into a three-tier system.

Answer: B

18. A travel company re-architects its application from a two-tier to a three-tier architecture. To see what impact the new architecture has on its non-functional requirements (NFR), the company intends to build a prototype based on the new architecture. The company compares the NFR metrics associated with the new prototype against the metrics from their original two-tier solution. Which option is an advantage of the original two-tier solution?

A. It has better availability because it has fewer single points of failure.

B. It has better manageability because each client has its own copy of the application.

C. It has better performance because each client must use its own set of domain objects.

D. It has better scalability because each client can access the database independently of other clients.

Answer: A

19. Which two statements describe the contact between an Enterprise JavaBeans (EJB) container and the EJBs that it hosts?

A. The container provides automatic logging of all exceptions and errors generated by EJB code.

B. The container provides a transparent scaling mechanism to handle spikes in demand.

C. An EJB can extend its services, such as security, to improve performance.

D. The container has a well-defined lifecycle model for each EJB type.

Answer: D

20. What are two consequences of using the Composite View pattern?

A. Improves performance

B. Avoids duplicate content

C. Forces a whole-part dependency

D. Al ows tables to be reused in multiple locations

E. Restricts all sub views to have a consistent view technology

Answer: B, D

21. Which option describes the design relationship between session beans and entity beans?

A. Aggregation

B. Separation of concerns

C. Common reuse principle

D. Liskov substitution principle

E. Interface segregation principle

Answer: B

22. Which three web applications work best when they are designed to be server-push enabled?

A. A news feed used for providing users with frequently updated news content

B. A web chat that allows users to communicate using easily accessible web interfaces

C. A live sporting event application, used to deliver current results during matches

D. An auction system that provides users with live online bidding

E. A graphics rendering application that generates visuals in an orderly fashion

Answer: A, B, D

23. A manufacturing company has a large investment in a legacy Inventory Management System (IMS) developed with third-party technologies. You have been asked to design a Java EE application that interacts with it. You would like to ensure the following:

-Minimal application code is required to parse the communication messages.

-Communication is asynchronous and stateless.

-Performance import of the existing system is minimal.

Which two technologies combined would meet these requirements?

A. XML

B. JSON

C. RMI

D. JAX-RS

E. JAX-WS

Answer: B

24. You need to restrict access to the administration screens in your website.Which two techniques test a user's permissions before granting access to a particular screen?

A. Enterprise JavaBeans (EJB) entity

B. Servlet filter

C. Custom tag library

D. Deployment descriptor

E. Custom JavaScript in JSP

Answer: A, D

25. A company is extending is successful social networking site to support the following channels: instant messaging (IM), email messaging and text messaging/SMS. At present, the site has scaled 400% in one year using a standard MVC Web framework the application experiences large surges or spikes in demand and also periods of inactivity. Notification delivery to the three channels does

not need to be guaranteed. Which solutions extends the current architecture and best meets the company's requirements?

A. Send the notification inline, that is, within the normal HTTP request-response cycle.

B. Place messaging on a Java messaging Service (JMS) queue and use message-driven beans (MDBs) to create and send notifications.

C. Insert the messages into a database and use plain old Java Objects (POJOs) to read the messaging using JDBC and send notifications.

D. Insert the messages into a database and use entity beans to read the messages using JDBC and send notifications.

Answer: B

26. Which two are objectives of the Strategy pattern?

A. To provide a way to configure a class with one of many behaviours

B. To define an object that encapsulates how a set of objects interacts

C. To define the skeleton of an algorithm, deferring some steps to subclasses

D. To decouple an abstraction, horn its implementation so that the two can vary independently

E. To define a family of algorithms, encapsulate each one, and make them interchangeable

F. To allow subclasses to redefine certain steps of an algorithm without changing the algorithm's structure

Answer: A, E

27. A company must honour a service-level agreement (SLA) for its application, which states all database requests must execute within three seconds. Users complain that some requests take longer than five seconds to complete. You have been
contracted to fix the problem. Which course of action do you recommend?

A. Modify the program to implement multi-threading and an event-driven design.

B. Add servers to distribute the load.

C. Upgrade the application server and the operating system.

D. Define a plan for isolating the bottleneck, and define indicators that will measure performance under a test load.

Answer: D

28. Your CMC wants to move several web-based search applications to an AJAX model, hoping to improve user engagement with a browser experience that feels smaller and more responsive. Which identifies a drawback to consider when adopting an AJAX model to improve user experience?

A. Maintaining current performance could require more hardware.

B. Maintaining accessibility across clients may require more development.

C. Maintaining security within the page could be more difficult.

D. Maintaining page navigability for users would have to be re-evaluated.

E. Maintaining a scalable system could require redesigning applications.

Answer: C

29. You are designing a new subsystem to store and scratch for user commands in a fashion company's website. On class, Comment Manager, is responsible for accessing comment data and providing read-only access to other objects in the subsystem. Which two implementation details are necessary for the Comment manager class?

A. The storage mechanism implemented in Comment Manager must be private to CommentManager.

B. Al the accessor and mutator methods in CommentManager must have the static modifier in their declarations.

C. The comments must be assessable directly only within CommentManager.

D. CommentManager should be a singleton object.

Answer: C, D

30. You are the architect of a web application that uses JavaServer Faces (JSF) as a presentation tier for business processes coded as stateless session beans. When you add new code to the stateless session beans to address new accounting requirements, without changing the interface, you discover that the new business processes are being ignored by some of the JSF components. What might be the cause of this problem?

A. The presentation tier is relying on validation logic in the business tier.

B. The browser is caching out-of-date versions of the JSF components.

C. The business processes are not rigorously encapsulated in the session beans.

D. The new session beans have been deployed incorrectly, and proper deployment will resolve the problem.

Answer: C

31. You are the architect for a patient management system with an HTML UI. Currently, it is used by ward nurses who access the system using dockable tablet computers. The application uses the HttpSession object to store information. In phase two of the implementation, nurses will also have access through smart phones. These phones will use a native client rather than HTML and will access the same business logic using a Web service. Which two are optimal methods to manage conversational state in the new version of the system?

A. The HTML UI and native clients both use HttpSession objects.

B. The HTML UI and native clients both use stateful session beans.

C. The HTML UI and native clients both use stateless session beans.

D. The HTML UI uses an HttpSession object; native clients create a session management object.

E. The HTML UI and native clients both use singleton beans.

Answer: B, E

32. Which two statements are true about RESTful web services?

A. They can be both stateful and stateless.

B. They support the use of AJAX in web applications.

C. They are often similar than their Simple Object Access protocol (SOAP) equivalents.

D. They are independent of the transport protocol.

E. They support Remote Procedure Call (RPC) and message-Oriented Middleware (MOM) integration styles.

Answer: B, D

33. Which two statements apply to unsigned applets?

A. They can access the client file system.

B. They can connect to third-party servers.

C. They can connect to the originating host.

D. They can invoke public methods of applets on a page.

E. They can load native libraries.

Answer: C, D

34. Your company uses a payroll application that was developed using Java technologies. The company has acquired another company and plans to integrate its payroll process in existing application. You have been asked to implement this integration. You observe that the business logic adopted to calculate the payroll is different in both companies. Which design pattern would be most appropriate to use in this integration?

A. Strategy

B. Payload Extractor

C. Fly Weight

D. Composite

E. Service Locator

Answer: D

35. Which two statements are true about the timer service of a business component container?

A. Timed notifications for all types of session beans can be scheduled by using this service.

B. When the server is shut down, the timer is persisted automatically and becomes active again when the server is restarted.

C. Each instance of message driven beans has unique timers.When stateful session bean instance is removed, the container detaches the timers associated with the instance and allocates them to the new instance.

D. When a transaction is rolled hark, the timer creation within the transaction is also rolled back.

Answer: A, B

36. Which three actions restrict the ability of a web application to scale in response to load as additional computing resources are made available to it?

A. Implementing the Singleton pattern in the web tier

B. Implementing core business logic in the web tier

C. Implementing core business logic using stateless session beans

D. Storing users' session state in a database

E. Maintaining users' session state by using stateful session beans

Answer: A, C, E

37. Which type of application would benefit from using the Singleton pattern?

A. An application that interacts with external systems in serial fashion.

B. An application that interacts with external systems in parallel fashion.

C. A clustered application that can support 200 concurrent users.

D. An application that requires remote monitoring capabilities

Answer: D

38. You are conducting a security audit for a web application that uses URL rewriting. The application does not allow for user-generated content and is accessible only via secured VPN. Which two security threats would you prioritize in your audit?

A. SQL injection

B. Cross-site scripting

C. Parameter-site manipulating

D. Session hijacking

E. Denial-of-service attacks

Answer: B, C

39. A company wants to design an internal website for the purpose of managing its numerous social events. The site will not have heavy traffic, but will require state to be persisted in a database. You have been tasked to complete this action item in your spare time. Which two Java EE-based approaches are best suited for quick development?

A. Use JPA in the web tier only.

B. Use message-driven beans to manage the posting of events.

C. Use your domain model components as JavaServer Faces (JSF) managed beans.

D. Use an Enterprise javaBeans (EJB) container to service-inject the domain model and support a JPA deployment.

Answer: A, C

40. Which three statements are true about inheritance?

A. Inheritance helps to reuse existing code implementations.

B. It should be possible to substitute the derived class for its base class.

C. Inheritance allows you to modify the behavior of objects.

D. Inheritance promotes encapsulation better than interfaces.

E. The derived class must override all methods of the base class.

Answer: A, C, D

41. Blue Berry Corporation, one of the biggest fruit traders in Canada, has the biggest competitor, Red Cherry Corporation. Blue Berry uses a web application that is developed by using java technologies, whereas Red Cherry's web application uses non-Java technologies. Blue Berry plans to share business sensitive, transactional data between the two systems by integrating them in a loosely coupled manner. Which technology should be used to this?

A. JMS

B. JCA

C. XML over HTTPS

D. RMI over IIOP

E. JBI

Answer: A, C

42. Which two actions limit the consequences of a network based attack?

A. Implementing the principle of least privilege

B. Installing a firewall at the outer boundary of your systems

C. Placing Internet-accessible servers in a demilitarized zone

D. Deploying a single sign-on system to provide system-wide authorization

E. Al owing application servers privileged access to all databases

Answer: B, E

43. You are implementing an online music that wil store and play a user's collection of songs. You want users to rate their songs and view the top songs from friends. Al queries must complete in

four seconds or less. Which approach would meet the response time requirement with minimal overhead?

A. Java class that uses JDBC with embedded SQL

B. Java class that uses an optimized stored procedure

C. JPA entity class with a lazy fetching strategy

D. JPA entity class with an eager fetching strategy

Answer: B

44. You are the architect of a JEE-based product that customers can configure to meet their own security requirements. You want to enforce basic without sacrificing customers ability to customize the product. Which is the best method to support both requirements?

A. Define base roles and users declaratively

B. Define base roles and users programmatically

C. Build a custom security service to handle authorization

D. Customize the JRE sandbox model by using local variables

Answer: D

45. You are the operations architect for a large online retailer. During peak times, your set of monitored applications exhibits non-reproducible errors. The data center is growing at 50% per annum, while your team headcount remains constant. Which method would you use to implement an affective monitoring strategy?

A. Use the Visitor pattern to collect per-JVM statistics and store them centrally.

B. Use the Strategy pattern to encapsulate collection logic for each JVM.

C. Use the Thread Tracker to monitor the JVMs directly.

D. Use the Observer pattern to monitor each JVM directly.

Answer: B

46. You are consulting with a team that has maintained several legacy database for years. They have reviewed the JPA spec and are wondering if the technology would offer benefits over this current SQL base. Which statement identifies a risk of adopting JPA?

A. JPA only works with wel -known data models.

B. JPA may be able to model every table as a class.

C. JPA could render code that requires extensive SQL tuning to perform well.

D. JPA's query language relies on a container to manage the persistence layer.

E. JPA doesn't provides ACID semantics.

Answer: D

47. Which two functions are essential parts of a service oriented architecture (SOA) infrastructure?

A. The service provider, which executes business logic in a stateless fashion

B. The service consumer, which accesses services from the service repository

C. The service repository, which stores software component metadata

D. The service broker, which delivers wel -defined service-level agreements

E. The service look-up facility, which provides a central resource for naming and access

Answer: A, C

48. A business application that runs in an Enterprise JavaBeans (EJB) container must communicate with a transactional third-party service. The communication technology must allow changing service providers without changing the application's business model. Which technology would meet these requirements?

A. Java Message Service

B. Remote Method Invocation

C. Simple Object Access Protocol

D. Java Connector Architecture

E. Java Business Integration

Answer: A

49. Which three principles are best practices when implementing a logging strategy for an enterprise application?

A. Never print log messages to the console window.

B. Use the appropriate logger level for logging information.

C. Log messages for every method entry and exit.

D. Include programmer-specific data in the log messages.

E. Include the thread name and Java class name in log messages.

Answer: B, C, D

50. Which two are primary concerns for a service-oriented architecture (SOA)?

A. Low cohesion

B. Loose coupling

C. Session handling

D. Wel defined contracts

Answer: B, D

51. Your company is considering migrating a persistence module, originally implemented as CMP entity beans, to now use JPA. Which two statements are true?

A. Each CMP entity bean can be mapped to a single JPA entity class.

B. The client code that accesses the CMP entity beans does not have to change.

C. IPA cannot capture all the kinds of relationships supported by CMP entity beans.

D. The resulting IPA persistence module can be used on both the client and the server.

E. The JNDI name of a JPA entity class can be customized to match that of the corresponding CMP entity bean.

F. Remote clients of the CMP entity beans must start using web services to access the JPA entity classes on the server.

Answer: B, D

52. Which two are significant advantages of developing web applications with JavaServer Faces (JSF)?

A. JSF pages can be previewed outside the web container.

B. Backing beans can be unit tested outside the web container.

C. Client-side validation mechanisms are automatically generated.

D. JSF pages can be integrated with AJAX.

Answer: A, C

53. Which three actions represent best practices when implementing an exception-handling strategy for an application?

A. Always include information specific to the error when logging an exception.

B. Always log the specific exception before re-throwing a wrapped exception.

C. Always throw exceptions in methods that are designed for exception handling.

D. Create a custom unchecked exception if the action to resolve the exception cannot be defined.

Answer. B, D

54. Your application uses web services extensively and frequently to distribute large XML objects over HTTP. In addition, the application has been set particularly demanding performance and scalability service level agreements (SLAs). Which java API is best suited for your application?

A. JAXB

B. JAXR

C. STAX

D. DOM

Answer: C

55. Which two statements are true about delegation as an Object-Oriented Design technique?

A. In Java technology, it is always implemented through the use of generics.

B. It allows you to replace Inheritance with composition.

C. It always requires that at least two objects are involved in handling a request.

D. It is applied to a system only at compile time.

E. It is an essential element of the Singleton pattern.

Answer: B, C

56. You are integrating with a single legacy Enterprise Information System. You are interested in the transaction management capabilities of Java Connector Architecture. This new system needs the capability to invoke multiple operations against this single legacy system. These operations succeeded together or fail together as a group. To which minimum level of transaction management do you set your resource adapter?

A. Distributed transaction

B. Local transaction

C. No transaction

D. Container-managed transaction

Answer: B

57. A company provides call center support for corporations world-wide. Each agent in the call center can be assigned to multiple call center customers. All the company's customers use Windows based user interfaces and it has Just signed a new customer that uses a Java EE back end and wants a rich interface. The company is developing a user interface for the new customer with the following requirements:

-Customer service representatives (CSRs) must be able to work with minimal training on the application.

-CSRs must be able to switch between call center systems quickly.

-Screens must have windows look and feel. -2000 agents spread across four locations must be able to use the system.

Which recommendation would you make to this company about the user interface (Ul)?

A. Write the Ul using AJAX, Accessing servlets directly.

B. Write the Ul using JSPs with embedded script lets.

C. Write the Ul usingJava Swingand describe using JNLP.

D. Write the Ul using JSP and JSTL.

Answer: C

58. StockTeller is a Java-based application designed to retrieve the current market for a portfolio of publicly listed stocks. You have been tasked to design a bolt on module for StockTeller called EBroker, a Java E-based online application that needs to asynchronously communicate with StockTeller to retrieve market prices for securities in a secure manner. Which web service technology would you choose to integrate StockTeller into the EBroker application?

A. JAX-WS using HTTPS

B. JAX-RS using HTTPS

C. JAX-RPC using HTTP

D. JAX-WS using HTTP

Answer: A

59. Your application produces messages by client applications. The number of clients interested in the messages varies continuously at run time. Any client can process any message, but a message must be processed exactly once. How should the messages be delivered to the clients?

A. Using XML over HTTP

B. Using a Java Message Service (JMS)queue

C. Using a Simple Object Access Protocol (SOAP) web service

D. Using a Java Message Service (JMS) topic

Answer: B

60. Which two security threats are negated by encrypting network transactions with Transport Layer Security (TLS)?

A. Cross-site scripting

B. Denial of service

C. Session hijacking

D. Man in the middle

E. SQL injection

Answer: C, D

61. A travel company re-architects its application from a two-tier to a three-tier architecture. To see what impact the new architecture has on its non-functional requirements (NFR), the company intends to build a prototype based on the new architecture. The company compares the NFR metrics associated with the new prototype against the metrics from their original two-tier solution. Which option is an advantage of the original two-tier solution?

A. It has better performance because each client must use its own set of domain objects.

B. It has better manageability because each client has its own copy of the application.

C. It has better scalability because each client can access the database independently of other clients.

Answer: B

62. Your CMC wants to move several web-based search applications to an AJAX model, hoping to improve user engagement with a browser experience that feels smaller and more responsive. Which identifies a drawback to consider when adopting an AJAX model to improve user experience?

A. Maintaining accessibility across clients may require more development.

B. Maintaining a scalable system could require redesigning applications.

C. Maintaining page navigability for users would have to be re-evaluated.

D. Maintaining securitywithin the page could be more difficult.

E. Maintaining current performance could require more hardware.

Answer: D

63. Which statement is true about the use of security-related annotations in an enterprise bean?

A. They can be used to change an authentication mechanism.

B. They can be used to acquire a secure connection using SSL

C. They can be used to specify permissions on a class or its business methods.

D. They can be inherited from a parent abstract class.

E. They can be used to specify permissions only on business methods.

Answer: C

64. You are the architect at ACME, a large global retailer of festival and holiday accessories. ACME wants to launch a new shopping portal for the holiday shopping session, allowing two months from project inception to going live. The portal must contain in-house and third-party stock to attack customers. Fast response times are also critical so users remain engaged and sticky to the portal. What would you recommend to the ACME project team to deliver this project?

A. Access all content regardless of source using the HTML 5 XML parsing capabilities of the browser

B. Access all third-party content using JSON to dynamically load it from the browser.

C. Access as much content with bulk-loading as possible; use JSONP to access the remainder.

Answer: C

65. You are designing a bank application in which automated email reminders are sent to customers every 24 hours, starting from five days prior to a payment due date until the payment is made? Which type of beans most closely match the implementation needs for this requirement?

A. Stateful session bean

B. Stateless session bean

C. Message-driven bean

D. Managed bean

Answer: C

66. You are asked to propose a software deployment strategy that will reduce a client make deploying and testing their software stack more efficient. Which element would you include in your proposal?

A. Vertically scalable platform

B. Horizontally scalable platform

C. Standard unit testing software

D. Virtualized platform

Answer: D

67. You are consulting with a team that has maintained several legacy database for years. They have reviewed the JPA spec and are wondering if the technology would offer benefits over this current SQL base. Which statement identifies a risk of adopting JPA?

A. JPA only works with well-known data models.

B. JPA doesn't provides ACID semantics.

C. JPA may be able to model every table as a class.

D. JPA could render code that requires extensive SQL tuning to perform well.

E. JPA's query languagerelies on a container to manage the persistence layer.

Answer: D

68. Which two statements are true about Java Cryptography Architecture (JCA)?

A. Categories of algorithms supported by JCA include message digests, signatures encryption, management, and random number generation.

B. Exactly one Implementation of each category of cryptographic algorithms must be provided.

C. Any JCA provider must implement each supported category of algorithms.

D. Implementations of cryptographic algorithms can be plugged in to a JVM after it has been installed and at run time.

Answer: A, D

69. Which two measures are most effective in protecting websites from cross site scripting (XSS) attacks?

A. Ensure that thesession cookie is sent only onHTTPSconnections.

B. URL-encode and ">"parameters so they will never be evaluated by the JavaScript Interpreter.

C. Treat all user-supplied input as unsafe, and white list known good characters

D. Execute all user-supplied scripts in aserver-side sandbox.

E. Escape "<" and ">" parameters that displayed or evaluated by the JavaScript interpreter.

Answer: A, D

70. You are the architect of an application that reads from and writes to multiple systems. The application must participate in an existing transaction to update a database using JDBC, and also invoke a transactional method on a remote system as part of the same transaction. Which two technologies would you suggest, to access remote system, for this application?

A. Simple Object Access Protocol (SOAP)

B. Remote Method Invocation (RMI)

C. Java Message Service (JMS)

Answer: A, C

71. You are contracted to improve the performance of an application. While analyzing the application, you observe the following issues:

-Tight coupling between client and business objects

-Too many remote method Invocations between client and server

Which design pattern is best suited to improving performance?

A. Web Service Broker

B. Session Facade

C. Value List Handler

D. Data Access Object

E. Service Activator

Answer: B

72. Your company has been using the ACME database vendor for many years. Recently, it started considering a migration to the XYZ database vendor, who uses different SQL dialect. The SQL engines in ACME and XYZ have significant differences in performance when executing the same SQL queries? Which is the best persistence technology for database migration?

A. JDBC

B. JPA

C. JDBC row set XML serialization

D. CMP entity bean

Answer: B

73. Which two use cases are best suited to the RPC style of messaging using Simple Object Access Protocol (SOAP)?

A. Executing long running multi-part processes

B. Implementing asynchronous web services

C. Implementing line grained services

D. Processing large sized communication messages

E. Validating custom data types

Answer: C, E

74. Blue Berry Corporation, one of the biggest fruit traders in Canada, has the biggest competitor, Red Cherry Corporation. Blue Berry uses a web application that is developed by using java technologies, whereas Red Cherry's web application uses non-Java technologies. Blue Berry plans to share business sensitive, transactional data between the two systems by integrating them in a loosely coupled manner. Which technology should be used to this?

A. JCA

B. JBI

C. XML over HTTPS

D. JMS

E. RMI over IIOP

Answer: A

75. A manufacturing company has a large investment in a legacy Inventory Management System (IMS) developed with third-party technologies. You have been asked to design a Java EE application that interacts with it.

You would like to ensure the following:

-Minimal application code is required to parse the communication messages.

-Communication is asynchronous and stateless.

-Performance import of the existing system is minimal.

Which two technologies combined would meet these requirements?

A. JSON

B. RMI

C. JAX-RS

D. XML

E. JAX-WS

Answer: A, C

76. Your company is creating a Java EE corporate wide workflow system in which significant internal business events are consumed by multiple applications. Due to multi-year development plans, many of these applications do not exist yet, even at the design stage. IT has defined standard data formats for these events in the form of small XML documents. Also, the rules for how an application filters and processes events are not fixed In advance and can change over the life of the application. Which combination of technologies is best for distributing and consuming these events throughout the company?

A. JMS queues and message-driven beans

B. Java Message Service (JMS)topics and message-driven beans

C. Remote Method Invocation (RMI) and stateless session beans

D. HTTP client library and servlets

E. Relational database and JDBC

Answer: B

77. Which two are primary concerns for a service-oriented architecture (SOA)?

A. Well defined contracts

B. Session handling

C. Loose coupling

D. Low cohesion

Answer: A, C

78. Which four services are guaranteed to be present in a specification compliant Java EE container?

A. Persistence

B. Naming and messaging

C. Remote connectivity

D. Failover

E. Lifecycle management

F. Multithreading handling

G. Load balancing

Answer: A, B, D, F

79. Your company has decided to expose a set of business operations through an API so that clients can access them remotely. These operations, which are modelled as methods on a stateless session bean component, act as building blocks for complex state-changing activities that need to possess atomicity,, consistency, isolation and durability (ACID) semantics. Select the best technology to implement the API.

A. Java Connector Architecture (JCA)

B. Remote Method Invocation (RMI)

C. Java Message Service (JMS)

D. XML over HTTP

Answer: B

80. You are the architect for XYZ bank. XYZ is redesigning their online banking offering and you need to ensure that the new design follows security best practices for the JEE platform. Select three security best practices for JEE applications.

A. Schedule regular penetration testing.

B. Log all security related application events.

C. Implement an exception-handling strategy.

D. Encrypt data, both on the wire and at rest.

E. Use both programmatic and declarative security.

F. Treat users as untrusted even when authenticated.

Answer: B, C, E

81. Which two statements are true about transport-layer security?

A. It is loosely coupled with the transport-layer protocol.

B. It is an end-to-end security mechanism.

C. It prevents the captured data from being replayed at a later time.

Answer: A

82. ABC Travel offers a night reservation service, exposed as a web service. XYZ Stays offers a hotel reservation service, also exposed as a web service. ABC and XYZ will not change their web service. A startup company has contacted you for advice about designing a new service that combines flight and hotel reservations, which they will offer as a web service. The startup company plans to provide their service by implementing a portable Java EE solution that aggregates the two services offered by ABC Travel and XYZ Stays, a combined reservation succeeded Only if both the flight reservation and the hotel reservation succeed. Which is the most effective way to meet the business requirement?

A. The startup company should implement their new service as a web service that uses an XA transaction manager.

B. The startup company cannot implement their new service as a web service, but must use an enterprise JavaBean (EJB) component to gain transaction propagation.

C. The startup company can implement their new service as a web service by calling the two existing services in a single transaction, relying on transaction propagation to support this business rule.

D. The startup company should implement their new service as a web service by calling the two existing services, and implementing their own compensating transaction.

Answer: D

83. Your company is considering migrating a persistence module, originally implemented as CMP entity beans, to now use JPA. Which two statements are true?

A. The JNDI name of a JPA entity class can be customized to match that of the corresponding CMP entity bean.

B. The resulting JPA persistence module can be used on both the client and the server.

C. JPA cannot capture all the relationships supported by CMP entity beans.

D. Remote clients of the CMP entity beans must start using web services to access the JPA entity classes on the server.

E. The client code that accesses the CMP entity beans does not have to change.

F. Each CMP entity bean can be mapped to a single JPA entity class.

Answer: B, F

84. A company must honour a service-level agreement (SLA) for its application, which states all database requests must execute within three seconds. Users complain that some requests take longer than five seconds to complete. You have been contracted to fix the problem. Which course of action do you recommend?

A. Upgrade the application server and the operating system.

B. Define a plan for isolating the bottleneck, and define indicators that will measure performance under a test load.

C. Modify the program to implement multi-threading and an event-driven design.

D. Add servers to distribute the load.

Answer: B

85. Blue Berry Corporation, one of the biggest fruit traders in Canada, has the biggest competitor, Red Cherry Corporation. Blue Berry uses a web application that is developed by using java technologies, whereas Red Cherry's web application uses non-Java technologies. Blue Berry plans to share business sensitive, transactional data between the two systems by integrating them in a loosely coupled manner. Which technology should be used to this?

A. XML over HTTPS

B. JMS

C. JCA

D. RMI over IIOP

E. JBI

Answer: C

86. Which two use cases are best suited to the RPC style of messaging using Simple Object Access Protocol (SOAP)?

A. Implementing asynchronous web services

B. Validating custom data types

C. Processing large sized communication messages

D. Executing long running multi-part processes

E. Implementing line grained services

Answer: B, E

87. Your web page design company is designing websites for all the stores in a local mall. Your company must create a consistent "look and feel" for these sites. After this "look and feel- project has gone through demonstration, enhancement and approval iterations with the malls. Lions, you job is complete and the development of the actual B2C (Business -to-Client) system will be handled by a different firm. Which architecture is most appropriate for your prototype project?

A. Three-tier, enterprise-centric

B. Three-tier, application-centric

C. Three, web-centric

D. Two tier, web-centric

Answer: D

88. A company that sells avatar skins to virtual reality environments has a static website for advertising their wares. The website was built using What You See Is What You Get (WYSIWYG) html editor and also contains a lot of JavaScript. The company now wants to add server-side processing capabilities developing a shopping application, the company is
considering using Java Server Faces (JSF) Which statement is true?

A. JSF tags cannot be integrated into the HTML generated by WYSIWYG editors.

B. The web pages cannot be previewed accurately with a generic WYSIWYG HIML editor.

C. The web pages must be converted into Face lets.

D. The JavaScript code has to be rewritten to conform to JSF standards.

Answer: B

89. Which two types of applications benefit from using Java Server Faces (JSF)?

A. An application that sets specific database validation listeners on a Ul component

B. An application with a customizable Ul skin

C. An application that implements access control on each action based on user role.

D. An application in which type conversion of the values of IJI components is implemented only in Java classes.

Answer: A, D

90. The integration team has reported a problem in testing a few deployed MDBs. By design, each MDB listens to one of four named queues. Two producers write messages to each queue. The test issues messages of the same payload type that each producer will send, but varies the number or size of these messages to measure the messaging server's performance. The team has noticed that the utilization remains at the same high rate any time the test writes messages destined for the third MDB. The message server log does not reveal any failure in sending messages to this MDB. Which anticipation expresses cause for this condition?

A. Hot Potato

B. Cache less Cow

C. Golden Hammer

D. Leaky Abstraction

Answer: A

91. Which three actions represent best practices when implementing an exception handling strategy for an application?

A. Create a custom unchecked exception if the action to resolve the exception cannot be defined

B. Always include information specific to the error when logging an exception.

C. Always log the specific exception before re-throwing a wrapped exception.

D. Always throw exceptions in methods that are designed for exception handling.

E. Create a custom checked exception if an alternative action can be taken to resolve the exception.

Answer: A, B, E

92. Your company provides a marketplace for industrial chemicals. You are required to offer accurate pricing and quantities to all marketplace users. Marketplace users are globally distributed. What is the most appropriate technology to use to satisfy this requirement?

A. An enterprise messaging system

B. Web services using REST

C. Client-side polling using JAX-RPC

D. Server-side distribution using JAX-WS

Answer: B

93. Which two kinds of applications benefit from the adoption of service-oriented architecture (SOA) inspired patterns and practices?

A. An application that utilizes fine-grained interfaces to provide communication to the object of a service

B. An application with tightly coupled services that enable messages to flow easily

C. An application in which the communication between services and the business process are platform independent.

D. An application that retains legacy systems while evolving to accommodate future business demands

Answer: C, D

94. Oasis Corporation has decided to develop a single Instance multi-tiered application with its existing EIS resources. You are the technical lead for the Integration team responsible for providing the following:

-A common Interface that can easily access the heterogeneous EIS resources

-Generic transaction mechanism support for EIS resource managers

-A connection pool to legacy EIS resources

Which two technologies would you use to meet these requirements?

A. JAX-WS

B. JDBC

C. JCA

D. JAX-RS

E. JMS

Answer: B, C

95. You are the architect for a patient management system with an HTML I-Jl. Currently, it is used by ward nurses who access the system using dockable tablet computers. The application uses the Http Session object to store information. In phase two of the implementation, nurses will also have access through smartphones. These phones will use a native client rather than HTML, and will access the same business logic using a Web service. Which two are optimal methods to manage conversational state in the new version of the system?

A. The HTML Ul and native clients both use stateless session beans.

B. The HTML Ul uses an HttpSession object, native clients create a session management object.

C. The HTML Ul and native clients both use HttpSession objects.

D. The HTML Ul and native clients both use stateful session beans.

E. The HTML Ul and native clients both use singleton beans.

Answer: B, D

96. During a security audit, it is noted that your application is vulnerable to SQL Injection attacks. Which two action would you perform to address this vulnerability?

A. Use parameterized stored procedures with the embedded parameters.

B. Configure security roles in the deployment descriptor.

C. Use parameterized stored procedures with the principle of least privilege.

D. Configure user permissions in the deployment descriptor.

E. Add a text input validation filter to check user-supplied data.

F. Deploy the Internet-facing nodes in a well-defined demilitarized zone (DMZ) layer.

Answer: A, C

97. While analysing an application, you observe that it contains numerous Interfaces for complex domain logic. Completing a business Function currently requires calling several of these interfaces in an order that is understood by system experts. Which design pattern would you suggest to refactor the code?

A. DAO

B. Decorator

C. MVC

D. Adapter

E. Façade

Answer: E

98. Which two are objectives of the Abstract Factory pattern?

A. To create families of related objects

B. To create whole-part hierarchies

C. To separate the construction of a complex object from its representation

D. To enforce dependencies between concrete classes

E. To specify the types of objects to create by using a sample instance

Answer: A, D

99. Which two statements are true about Java integration technologies?

A. Java Message Service (JMS) helps in synchronous messaging between Java and non-Java systems.

B. Java Connector Architecture (JCA) helps to integrate with heterogeneous legacy enterprise information systems.

C. Remote Method Invocation (RMI) helps to connect subsystems in a loosely coupled manner.

D. JMS helps to broadcast messages to multiple Java-based receivers.

Answer: B, D

100. You are the lead technical designer for a new B2C retail application. A key goal is to minimize design and build complexity in order to maximize speed to market. Which three features of JPA make it the most appropriate technology to use in building the persistence layer of the application?

A. JPA provides vendor-neutral database access

B. JPA ensures optimal database access logic

C. JPA ensures thread safe semantics

D. JPA does not require an EJB container

E. JPA provides transparent scalability

F. JPA provides ACID semantics

Answer: A, D, F

101. Your Docs is an application that retrieves PDF documents of selected topics from both trusted and untrusted websites. It has been developed using a non-Java technology. You are designing your Mlearn, a mobile-based e-learning application, which will be implemented in Java. You plan to integrate YourDocs with your application. Which web service technology would you choose to Integrate YourDocs into the Your MLearn application?

A. JAX-WS

B. JAX-WS with REST

C. JAX-RPC

D. JAX-RS

Answer: D

102. Upper management has announced a change in a company's primary hardware supplier for the next year, the timing of this change coincides with key purchases that line of business department has to make in support of its Java EE application upgrade/redesign project. You are asked to help outline a strategy to preserve the project timeline and keep hardware training costs contained. Which recommendation will you make?

A. Use new hardware on the web tier and redeploy existing hardware to the other tiers.

B. Request more time to consider the total cost of change to your project and to modify your budget.

C. Request another year of sales and support with the existing vendor.

D. Add new hardware to create a heterogeneous environment.

Answer: D

103. You are designing a new subsystem to store and scratch for user commands in a fashion company's website. On class, Comment Manager is responsible for accessing comment data and providing read-only access to other objects in the subsystem. Which two implementation details are necessary for the Comment Manager class?

A. All the accessor and mutator methods in Comment Manager must have the static modifier in their declarations.

B. The comments must be assessable directly only within Comment Manager.

C. Comment Manager should be a singleton object.

Answer: A, C

104. Which two types of applications benefit from using Java Server Faces (JSF)?

A. An application with a customizable UI skin

B. An application that implements access control on each action based on user role.

C. An application in which type conversion of the values of UI components is implemented only in Java classes.

D. An application that sets specific database validation listeners on a UI component

Answer: C, D

ONLINE RESOURCES

Advanced Java Playlist:

Link : https://www.youtube.com/playlist?list=PLzlh_31VWEFoZXs-3KLPda_DVIN9IPJyg

QR Code :

Java Interview Playlist:

Link: https://www.youtube.com/playlist?list=PLzlh_31VWEFryjvGNIVtyBVYvddpxKexP

QR Code:

Java EE 7 Application Developer (Paper Code - 1Z0-900) Playlist.

Link: https://www.youtube.com/playlist?list=PLzlh_31VWEFodNsy-MeBm7RdKGWAO4TzF

QR Code:

Oracle Certified Professional Java Programmer OCPJP (Paper Code - 1Z0-809) Playlist.

Link: https://www.youtube.com/playlist?list=PLzlh_31VWEFqzXoVrZjKV6cZQKi7iG2D9

QR Code:

Oracle Certified Master Java Enterprise Architect (OCMJEA)(Paper Code - 1Z0-807) Playlist.

Link: https://www.youtube.com/playlist?list=PLzlh_31VWEFqdceCx1Pivwi5ypdvfVaEs

QR Code:

Oracle Certified Master Java Enterprise Architect (OCMJEA)(Paper Code - 1Z0-807) Playlist.

Link: https://www.youtube.com/playlist?list=PLzlh_31VWEFr90bIgv56c3xabjV50iFLV

QR Code:

Core Java Textbook Playlist.

Link:

https://www.youtube.com/playlist?list=PLzlh_31VWEFofK7phOZSB9OO9rP1bkaxB

QR Code:

Printed at Repro India Ltd.